Usborne

Art Nouveau patterns to colour

Illustrated by Mary Kilvert and Emily Beevers
Written by Emily Bone

Art Nouveau patterns

Art Nouveau is an ornate design style made up of curved lines and stylized plants and animals. French for 'new art', it became popular in Europe at the end of the 19th century and was very different from existing art and design.

Natural art

Art Nouveau artists and designers were inspired by things in nature. Patterns had bold, simplified flowers on twisting stems and vines. Many patterns featured insects and birds, too.

Soft pastel colours, such as turquoise, purple, pink and pale blue were mixed with gold and black.

Flowers with soft petals and long stems, such as poppies, were popular.

Peacocks and peacock feathers were used in many designs.

Art Nouveau-style butterfly with patterned wings

Vine and leaf patterns were made into decorative borders.

Nouveau fashion

Many fashion designers were influenced by Art Nouveau. Dresses were made in loose shapes, and fabric was printed or embroidered with Art Nouveau patterns.

Accessories were small and delicate. Many were made to look like insects or flowers.

Hats were often decorated with flowers and feathers.

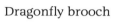

Dragonfly brooch

Evening coat with flower print from 1912

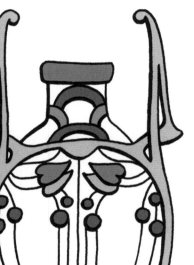

Outside and in

Buildings were designed with decorative windows and doors. Vases, glassware and other everyday objects were made in unusual shapes and painted with patterns.

This Art Nouveau vase has a stand and handles shaped like a climbing vine.

Advert art

Advertisements had bold type and striking patterns or figures done in an Art Nouveau style.

This distinctive Art Nouveau-style type is taken from an advertisement for soap.

SAVON

Flower art

Simplified, repeated flowers were popular patterns
for textiles and interiors. Artists often painted
women surrounded by flowering vines or garlands.

This dress is decorated with a pattern that looks a bit like an Indian vine. Colour it gold, pink and purple.

Turquoise wide-brimmed hat with gold feathers and red roses

Nouveau accessories

Accessories decorated with ornate flowers, insects or birds added elegant Nouveau touches to fashionable outfits.

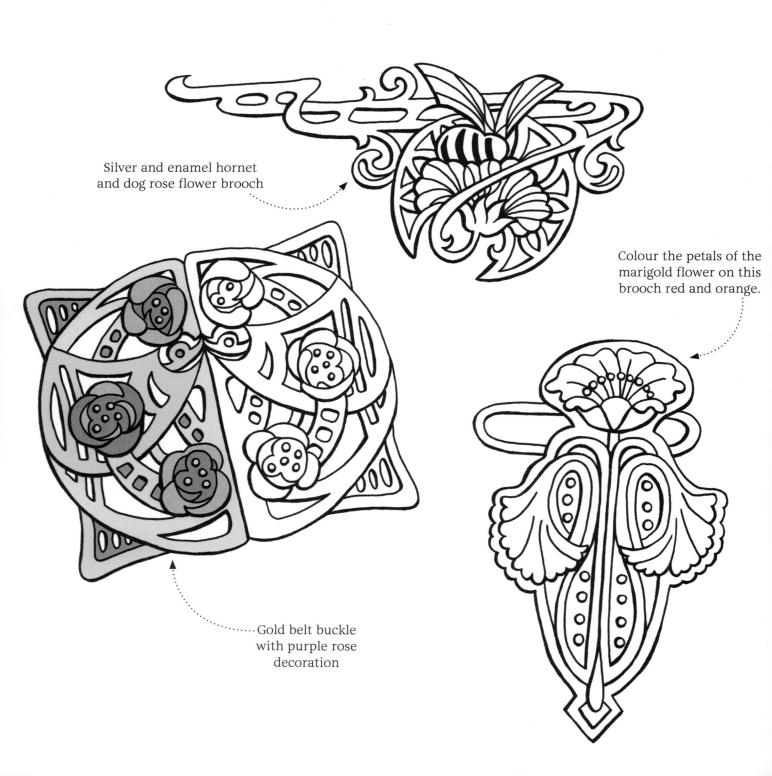

Silver and enamel hornet and dog rose flower brooch

Colour the petals of the marigold flower on this brooch red and orange.

Gold belt buckle with purple rose decoration

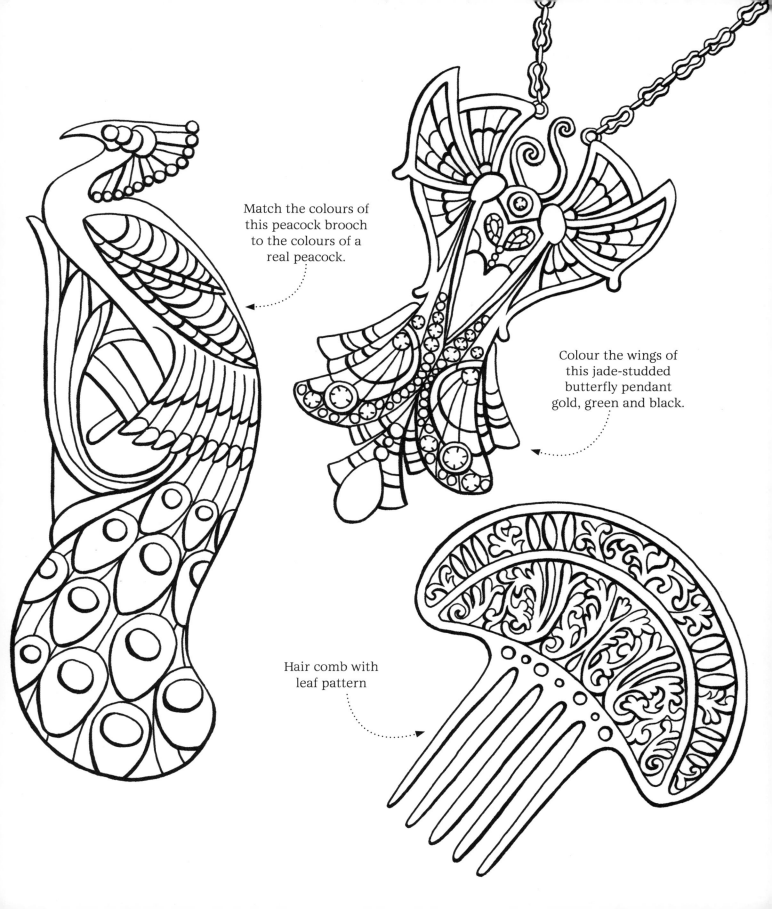

Match the colours of this peacock brooch to the colours of a real peacock.

Colour the wings of this jade-studded butterfly pendant gold, green and black.

Hair comb with leaf pattern

Nouveau home

Plates and vases had gently curved outlines and were
decorated with Art Nouveau patterns.

This vase is shaped like a
bunch of lily flowers.

The base and handles
on this vase are
designed to look like
leaves and vines.

Beautiful buildings

Streets in some European cities, such as Paris, Brussels, Budapest and Vienna, were lined with stunning Art Nouveau buildings. They had ornate windows and doors, and highly patterned bricks and tiles.

This door is surrounded
by twisting lines of metal,
called wrought iron.

Glamorous glass

Some Art Nouveau buildings were designed with
beautiful stained glass windows.

Use bright colours to
fill in these lampshades,
as though the light is
shining through them.

Arty adverts

Advertisements from the Art Nouveau period were designed in a flat style with patterned borders and bold, distinctive type. These posters are advertising perfume and soap.

CLUB DE DANSE

Clubs commissioned artists to create striking posters promoting shows and star performers.

Nouveau Japanese

Many designers looked to traditional Japanese art for inspiration. These Art Nouveau designs use Japanese clothing, flowers and birds.

The swirling line patterns in both these pictures are designed to look like rippling water.

First published in 2014 by Usborne Publishing Ltd, Usborne House, 83-85 Saffron Hill, London EC1N 8RT, England. www.usborne.com